MY CHIMERA

Michael Penny

BuschekBooks
Ottawa

Library and Archives Canada Cataloguing in Publication

Penny, Michael, 1952-
    My chimera / Michael Penny.

Poems.
ISBN 1-894543-34-3

    1. Animals--Poetry. I. Title.

PS8631.E572M9 2006   C811'.6   C2006-901845-6

Printed by Hignell Book Printing, Winnipeg, Manitoba.

BuschekBooks
PO Box 74053, 5 Beechwood Avenue
Ottawa, Ontario K1M 2H9
Canada

BuschekBooks gratefully acknowledges the support of
the Canada Council for the Arts for its publishing pro-
gram.

Canada Council   Conseil des Arts
for the Arts   du Canada

To Virginia, Emily, and Jane, My All.

TABLE OF CONTENTS

ACKNOWLEDGMENTS

Some of these poems appeared in *The New Quarterly* and were broadcast on CBC. Thanks to them. Thanks also to Bert Almon, Kimmy Beach, Olga Costopoulos, Lee Elliot, Shawna Lemay, and Iman Mersal, whose comments on these poems improved them. Thanks finally to John Buschek, a true friend of Canadian poetry. Finally, any errors in Zoology remain those of the author.

MY TRILOBITE

refuses to acknowledge
extinction,
its antennae wildly seeking tomorrow.

My three-lobed creature
may be imbedded in limestone
that's lasted 400 million years

but it notes its insect descendants
("friends & colleagues," it says)
now rule the Earth.

My trilobite was the earliest
animal with eyesight,
so it should see its dilemma—

mere imprint in stone—
but no, it's just a phase
this being a fossil.

MY VIRUS

lives on an earth made
to support its shell as hard
as the crust of that earth.

It falls into my soft biology
as easily as a stone into water
doing as much good as that stone.

What is the water's response
to the stone?
But my virus is unemotional

hard-headed, you'd say
if heads came into it.
It's an alive particle determined

to make other particles, so genuinely
unconcerned about what on earth it is.
Reflection is a nasty habit.

MY BUG

never tells me its name,
not even its last one.
Won't be friend enough for first.

There's probably a couple
of Latin ones even it
doesn't know.

But it's attracted to my writing
light, this dark evening,
and erratically comments.

It has wings—I can hear
the buzz, and feel
it randomly hit my face.

A body, and likely legs
to negotiate ground.
It might have sins and graces,

but it lands once too often
on my page. The side of my fist
and it's a grey-brown blot.

It's an instinct
this smudging hand,
for both it and me.

MY MAGGOT

has a single mantra
and it's "eat, eat, and eat"
especially of what used to eat.

Its theology is simple:
eat or be eaten
and a crowd is better.

My maggot, blind
lump,
might see the clearest—

as it ingests its way
to reincarnation, the blue jewel
of the fly it will become.

MY TAPEWORM

wears a hat with hooks
on its small head
to grasp the intestine

where it lives blind
in a constant flow
of food and comfort.

It's mostly tail
and eggs for more tapeworms
and couldn't enjoy life more.

My tapeworm wriggles
there's enough food for it
and its animal apartment.

Who's to criticize
this complete philosopher
in its best of all possible worlds?

MY SNAIL

is homeless;
it does look housed,
hard-shelled and spiral.

It can retreat into its curves
but that's no place to live.
It's a true peripatetic

looking for a place
to pitch its mostly hollow shell.
(Empty is easier to carry.)

Eyes on stalks to see the whole world,
but my snail knows if you can't leave it
it couldn't have been home.

MY SLUG

is slow: but it's a marathon
destroying my lettuce
chasing down the pea leaves

before there's blossom.
Massage earth with your belly
and it will supply.

As nothing runs away
it takes its time, making extra
slime to paint the world.

I have to work quickly to live
it seems, so have no time
to build silver highways,

but then, who predicts the anger,
the boot-heel or even the frothy death
from the salt shaker?

MY WORM

turns.
What ambition causes it to process soil
in the hole it makes in that soil?

My worm digests my planet
as it weaves through the roots
of my garden.

I bless it, believing worms
are good for gardens
but I especially like their silence.

It would be unbearable
to hear that underground
squeeze and slide.

My spade accidentally
cuts one into a squirm
that looks like screaming.

I am told, but do not believe,
those parts will become
two new worms

because I know I couldn't
pull off that trick,
disaster doubling to success.

MY SCORPION

is a dry wit
preferring desert
and making a home in sand.

If I turn over a loose rock
a desiccated leaf
it will be there and ready

to engage me in debate.
It knows its territory,
has counted the sparse issues

of its landscape
and ends all argument
with the sting in its tail.

MY CENTIPEDE

was an early convert
to the metric system,
as it's always measured its earth

a footstep at a time
(then dividing by one hundred)
to make its perfect survey.

Its map organises dinner,
this place for ants,
that for beetles

and under this dropped bark
all the soft worms its venom
will subdue to banquet.

You see, there's a sting
however you get there,
at the end of reckoning.

MY MILLIPEDE

is a night creature
you'd think was fast,
except it needs a thousand

places to put its feet.
Like most slower things
it's always scared.

Threatened, it burrows
into a getaway cave,
or emits evil-odoured poisons

which let you smell
it's not good to eat.
Mostly, though, at night

you'll find it rolled
into a chiton-plated ball
as round and solid as a moon.

MY COCKROACH

is as hard on its surface
as all the world
in which it lives

as it accommodates
what accommodates it.
It survives on what's given.

And its antennae
pick up everything
its mouth will pick up.

Surveillance is perfect
when you live hidden
in the muck in the corners.

MY FLEA

is large;
of course, everything's relative
but it pushes protein molecules around

its own quantum mechanics
meaning many straight lines
from random blood to random blood.

Fingernail hard, it's slippery
until it snuggles down
to form the deepest friendship.

I'm its blood brother
as it uses its smallness
to give nothing back.

MY ANT

is a series of black gems
lined up for a necklace
strung only by instinct.

I know an ant
is but part of Ant
and none will wink

at me as if to say
I'm just an atom
in a busy molecule

but look how glossy
the curves of my buff
carapace!

No, it's as unintelligent
as a gemstone, never
suffers being wrong,

a perfect black necklace
given to seduce Earth
into another bad affair.

MY MANTIS

prays upright;
it has knees and kneeling
and eyes big enough

to see God and victims.
It can even fly,
crinkly wings battering

sky into submission.
It values height, heaven
the tallest, thinnest twigs.

It's found a way to pray
while hunting, and
without supplication.

MY HOUSE-FLY

unavoidable glutton
proves I make garbage
and do so where I live.

Like most truth detectors,
it's metal, mostly chrome,
except for its crystal eyes

some diamond cutter
ground and polished
to meet light with perfection.

My house-fly turns on
those perfect eyes to find
all the shit in this world.

MY MOTH

is crepuscular;
its choice to be a moderate.
Uncomfortable

with both full dark and full light.
It's also self-conscious
drab and hairy

its fat feathered antennae
making it look
stubby.

My moderate, insecure moth
sleeps in, waking to a sun
with a bright bewilderment.

MY MOSQUITO

is a delicate machine
of fine levers and wings
as thin as its effective music.

It braces itself on my arm,
and I could brush it away,
or flatten it in a second.

I do nothing as it dips
into my skin, annoying me,
proving God is unbenevolent.

As if God noticed a slight swelling
and red itch. Instead, the devil is in
this detail of the universe,

which smears to a light black
when it bothers me and I
bother to bother it back.

MY CATERPILLAR

didn't work hard enough.
After its hard-shelled sleep my caterpillar
emerged simply as an older grub.

My caterpillar won't be consoled
that it's learned change does not
always follow unelaborated will

because it has butterfly dreams—
as it climbs the leaf it's chewing
its front legs reach for sky.

MY BEES

are filling my house.
They find the window open for in,
but cannot find the same window out—

my bees have failed basic navigation.
They buzz around, but they're lost
in drapes and vacuum cleaners.

Honeycombs grow in the corners
and my bees swarm the bathroom
at the most embarrassing times.

They still don't listen;
our only dialogue stings.
I grow lumpy with this conversation.

MY CRANEFLY

is an unfinished sketch of an insect
mostly legs like pencil lines
tentative on a white sky

but someone has also drawn
my cranefly wings like windows
open to that sky.

My cranefly tries all directions at once
this way, that, then the other,
convinced that random lines

make a life, but it will never
be sure. The pencil which made it
draws no conclusions.

MY GRASSHOPPER

lives with chaos.
It will orbit nothing
but instead jump

unpredictably
although mostly up.
My grasshopper, clumsy about direction

as it is strong about lift-off
bangs its legs on itself
and topples down.

My grasshopper is a quantum mechanic
repairing that leaky seal
between earth and sky.

MY CICADA

waits a winter, a summer,
each seventeen times
and then it's this one,

and the larva comes out
of its shell, and crawls up
into my world.

My cicada improvises music
takes out personal ads
to get dates and generally

spreads its wings, all
to begin a family—eggs
left in crevices in bark

to hatch into more larva,
which will wait again for
seventeen, that prime number.

MY WASP

finds me mowing the lawn,
when I brush against a branch
with an unfortunate paper fruit.

One sentinel rallies the nest
and buzzing like a beginner brass player
tracks down the shoulder which offended it.

My ill-aimed slap means a sting
in the palm of my hand, and my life-line
is now as bumpy as, well, my life.

I wish my wasp could see
it was another of my inadvertences,
how I'm really a swell guy.

MY BUTTERFLY

sprawls under a warm sun
like an open book
written in the characters

of a language unknown to me.
Can my butterfly read
its own message?

It does reassure me
there's a spine, and a tongue
to dip honey,

and long antennae, yes
sensitive enough to swivel back
and make out the text behind them:

it's code,
my butterfly says,
which only the sun can decipher.

MY GREEN ALGAE

is blue; the point of it
long ago perfected
by sunlight and water.

It would like to make something
of itself—only as much glory
as much food—

and gain some integrity.
After all, if you're big enough
to contain a nucleus....

Respect beginnings, define humble
with its name, that's true
complexity.

MY HORSESHOE CRAB

is not a crab
(nor horseshoe neither)
but metastomata, "legs joined to mouth."

My horseshoe crab crushes food
with leg spines which then lever it
through its jawless, speechless mouth.

It cannot insult, argue, or bless
this most wise and ancient creature
keeping that secret of survival.

MY BLUE CRAB

stuffed like that
in a hard shell so tight
it provokes headaches.

You'll see my crab's
estuarine scuttle
and think it pincers disdain

but its macroinvertibrate
self needs therapy.
My crab's eyes bulge

as it opens and closes
its constrained claws
signing, let me out.

MY JELLYFISH

is brainless
but still radially symmetric
as if to say:

come at me as you will
and it'll still be me.
It pulsates, rather than swims.

But my jellyfish gets what it wants
by waiting
tiny harpoons at the ready

for the gullible who come too close.
Brainless, it cannot deceive;
I can see right through it.

MY CORAL POLYPS

nearly always pay their rent
but with millions of tenants
some will forget.

Most are also recluses
whose tentative tentacles
hold nematocysts which barely sting.

They'll wait for food
or inspiration to come to them.
Some will be noisy

as even microscopic parties
with the right band will rock
the future limestone.

My coral polyps might each be insignificant
as a thought, but their persistence accretes
to form the hard reef on which I run aground.

MY HERMIT CRAB

is house hunting
for an eight claw unit
with room to spread antennae.

It's in the market for something used
perhaps a mollusk's estate sale
and, yes, definitely unfurnished.

My hermit crab's needs
are simple, but specific—
a home shell light enough to carry

but strong enough to believe in,
armour it won't grow for itself,
my sovereign of the second-hand.

MY GIANT CLAM

lives in corrugated stone
rippled like the ripples
of the sea around it.

It stays rooted to the reef
content to do nothing but grow
and siphon whole oceans for food.

It gapes, hinge downward
as if credulous at the activity
of the mobile around it.

My giant clam is proud
of its plush furnishings
(spotted purple velvet, no less)

and with such contentment
while staying still,
why make travel plans?

MY SEA URCHIN

attends its family reunion
of starfish, sand dollars,
and sea cucumbers,

each named for something
they're really not.
They console each other—

no backbone nor brain—
unable to ask
the Big Questions.

Am I wrong? As my sea urchin
with its thousand serious pencils
tries to write me an answer

on the endless pages
the sea makes, erases,
and makes again.

MY SQUID

is a winged jet
expelling water
to get through water.

It's wrapped around
what it moves through
as it has no there.

My squid is sudden;
having no destination
except away to hide

its journey with ink
that writes an itinerary
only as it erases.

MY OCTOPUS

takes eight steps at once
so eager to get to the centre
of things

as, with eight directions to go
it must seek a centre
to begin from.

My octopus has rows of lights
on tentacles supple enough
to make question marks

as it spreads and searches
the underwater rocks
for something to adhere.

MY FLOUNDER

has a rounded personality
as there's a surface to the earth
even under all the seas;

things inclined
to hide will tend toward it.
My flounder pretends like that,

just mud and sand and waste
until an eye opens or a fin twitches
and I've got it against the muck.

When your belly's mostly in mud
you need upward turning eyes
for the vague opportunity

and definite predator.
I know when I flounder around,
belly against the muck of days

I must look up and out
for what's coming
to catch me.

MY SARDINE

is no truant
attending school faithfully
to learn its only lesson:

be attentive to those around.
My sardine might lead a pelagic life
but it feels no freedom,

just millions like it
around it, being it
in the colder water.

My sardine is no rebel
but a silver crowd, close
and loyal, from egg to the can.

MY GOLDFISH

is fake;
an accurate scale
proves it's just brass

splashing around in
liquid diamonds
themselves just glass.

I know now it isn't
gulping,
but confessing.

MY FROG

misunderstands leap years,
used as it is to quick leaps
day to day through a life

for which an extra day means
performance of the usual tricks
of eating, sleeping, and making

new frogs, which also do not care
that, one in four, there's a stop
in the year's leap day to day

because the planet will not
multiply its own twirl
as it swings around the sun.

MY CHAMELEON

forgets its skin's ability
and believes the universe
changes to match it.

These changes are a perfect
discourse, a session which
replaces all the questions.

My chameleon answers a fly
with a sticky tongue rolling up
one movement down its throat

but to me it gives
soil, green branch and sky
each mirrored in its turning.

MY PYTHON

loves me so much
its affectionate hug
flattens lungs

and shatters my struggling bones
(Can you see those white
splinters through my skin?)

My python teaches me
becoming encoiled
doesn't always wrap things up.

MY GECKO

is attracted by the moths
attracted by the porch light
over this evening's door.

The moths are confused
at the new electric moon
which does not navigate them.

They whirr wings and legs
hoping the next direction
will make it all come right.

My gecko, hooked feet
running it upside down,
eyes bulging at the banquet

stops, watches, then leaps.
Another moth is gone, as my gecko
navigates it to its death.

MY RED-BELLIED BLACKSNAKE

is two-toned, sliding on its best part—
a crimson belly making no point
but don't step on its black back.

My hiking habit: step on
a log, not over it, until
I see what's over it.

It might be a previously calm snake.
Step on it, there's the sudden
red flag, the black muscle

and milky venom
the injection which inoculates
against life.

MY TYRANNOSAURUS

is grouchy
roaring down the days
of its extinction

because it sleeps so poorly.
When it dozes off,
it confronts two recurring dreams.

The first is of a sky
turning into black rock
as round and large as all daylight.

The second is this:
a crowd, a public place
but naked to its bones.

MY TORTOISE

My tortoise lives in a hard-floored hovel
but cramped just right.
All my houses should fit so well, if so tightly

it's a squeeze to get out to eat and fuck.
A perfect dwelling means
responsibility —

a simple stroll is a house-moving.
But the planet where it keeps its house
weighs down my accommodated tortoise

neck swayer, arthritic questioner
but with claws to grip the earth
like a foundation.

MY BIRD OF PARADISE

is legless and can't perch, so it flies
and floats against the dull overcast
of a tropical sky.

It lives in air,
eats just pollen and drinks clouds.
Its tail feathers glow with the effort.

Sometimes beautiful is just work
making all that colour
into radiant plumage.

Or energy grown massless
at a speed slower than light squared.
That same light

which victimizes into vision.
So I, two legs below, am a watcher,
flightless and unmagnificent.

MY SEAGULL

is a guru
denouncing this and that
lack of spirituality

in its accusatory squawk.
I once believed my seagull's
tone was merely angry—

if I insist on a beach-lunch
do I really have to throw
a french fry to it?

My seagull, wiser in spirit,
accepts each greasy enlightenment
with a demand for the next.

MY SPARROW

believes everything
is potentially edible
with a beak's try at it.

The key is quickness
a constant startle
and there's no escape.

It requires so much
to keep that heart and mind
jerking forward

under the feathered head
and lighter than air
attitude.

If you don't try it out
you can't tell
if you can eat it.

And my sparrow takes up
such small amounts of air,
but quickly.

MY HUMMINGBIRD

doesn't bother with words
for the fast melody
its flight sings.

It's not my tiny bird's choice
as blossoms schedule themselves
so tightly there's no time

to include their names
in its lyric.
It knows quickness counts

and, even as it avoids words
which might slow it down
it's still honey-tongued

and free, its needled beak
addressing but these two:
nectar, and now.

MY WOODPECKER

has a headache.
It still stands upright
beak tapper with a purpose

seeking insects and explanation
in the dead branches.
Why doesn't everything grow forever?

Is it because death
supports its own life
in the grubs chewing old wood

for a woodpecker to find
as it knocks and knocks
its sore head to no-one's answer?

MY RAVEN

Wing fingers measure the air
with a deliberate glide
then a bank to land.

Down here, it's mine
a beak into everything
from honey to carrion.

I find it in rocky landscapes
as if quartzite sharpened the beak
that comprehends the world.

A cloud or my interest
startles it, aching weightlifter
into the air.

Once again, it has fingers
and an accurate estimate
of what might fly.

MY PIGEON

My urban dove proves
you must like cities
for the scrounge.

Of course, it's mislead
by much of what's found
finally unnourishing;

it will try anything
like food so long as it spills
golden from trucks and stores.

The difficulty is my pigeon
must land near, and risk
cat, hawk, or predator cars.

A trick works only when
there's a victim,
so my pigeon must fall again

for the con-game of crowds,
the life of an unmediated
city, everything as it is.

MY OWL

needs eyeglasses
corrective vision to match
its swoop as silent as empty air

which will end in rodent
and the forked talons
it now stretches.

All flesh ends sooner
or later as fodder.
It's better to see that clear.

MY FLAMINGO

thinks upside-down,
a beady eye in its inverted
face daring me

to take it seriously.
I know nothing orange-pink
will discover new planets

but my flamingo
can lock its knee joints
whip its head around

and ask of salt marsh,
What have you fed me
lately, what's here for me?

MY EMU

sees better as it stretches its neck
sensing it should be skyward.
But its toes are too thick for take-off.

When it ruffles its lank feathers
it should be the downbeat for air
but it lopes away, looking past its wings

to say there's distinction
in two legs, in running.
Then its eyes give it away,

showing this bewilderment:
how can it be a bird
if it's truly flightless?

MY LOON

is sleek as water
made of the same smooth substance
and, at this moment, calm.

My loon is watching
not hunting
turning its eye this way,

that, over the surface
of the water which supports
its surface.

From the dry shore
I call it by its name;
itself, it's sure of its sanity.

MY PENGUIN

is cold
but need not waste heat
growing colourful.

Only black and white
as even grey is too equivocal
for a frozen world.

For six months it swims in ice
making little grace
from that absurdity.

No feathers, oily skin—
an evolutionary accident—
but why live anywhere cold?

Because the fish are free
and the tides keep it
safely near land.

MY DUCK

knows the best stuff is in mud
below muddy water.
A beak-load at a time

my duck eats another swamp
at the cost of full immersion
a surface fluster of feathers, water off.

Any pond bottom
is dead organic stuff
or simply shit

so it's good my duck flies.
My duck's triphibious
even if it's complicated

walking in water
swimming on land
but then flying, flying.

MY RED-TAILED TROPIC BIRD

treats the winds as an easy slope
to climb, or slide down
the blue,

the other blue which is not ocean.
It complains as I visit
its deserted (until me) desert island

of sandy nests
and dry crackling leaves
(the wind speaks frond.)

My red-tailed tropic bird
is mostly white, the other white
which is not coral sand,

but there's that red streamer of tail,
the flag of its territory
independent, reefed

and for which it has denied
my visa application.
I am an illegal in paradise.

MY CORMORANT

right now has its hooked beak
tucked under its wing
and the fishes sleep.

Soon its beady eye
will seek dinner and each
ripple becomes a menu item.

My cormorant is sleek
and, for something which flies,
can be fish-like in its dive

gulp and swallow.
Then it stands, wings akimbo
a drying cross on its rock.

MY BLUE JAY

is a paint-by-numbers bird,
blue here, black and white
(of course) and grey.

Two for blue, for sure,
and zero for white,
but black wants all the numbers.

Grey is a problem;
so soft and ambiguous
its number is the solution

to a tautology.
This concerns only me,
as my blue jay is ignorant

of math except the numbers
which allow arrogant flight
in a sky, two for blue.

MY BAT

hears what I can't see
on its perfect radar
when night makes its dark pictures

into which I step reluctantly
and with ancestral trepidation.
My bat, also a cave-dweller

like those who formed my fear,
will avoid me, I and my history
solid enough to reflect radar.

MY POSSUM

plays piano, dead
and a tough hand
of poker.

Piano, because it's a scamper
and climb, leaping
from one stave to the next.

"Dead."
Like all animals which live
mostly in the human night

it learns to play a mid-
roadway death perfectly.
As perfectly as it bluffs

its more animate attackers.
Thus all those pots won
ten high, the piano again.

MY MOLE

snouts the earth
whiskers exploring everywhere
as it searches

for new clay to colonise.
My mole makes empires
of oxygen-starved cellars,

and like all imperialists
solves the suffocation problem
with extra red blood cells.

MY DOLPHIN

is an acrobat
jumping and twisting
in the waves' passage

as if the tides, the swell
the whole transit of the ocean
came about to support it.

My dolphin competes
with air and gravity
and defeats them to be.

MY WHALE

wonders what land is.
The ocean gets shallow,
its dinner plate eyes

see bottom more clearly,
and it no longer needs
the deep breath for deep.

My whale might glimpse
a beach, a cliff, a volcano
in one of its breaches.

It doesn't know,
but thinks land is something
not as vast as what's around it,

that unbounded space
which convinces my whale
it is but a wet speck.

MY RHINO

is thin-skinned.
An egret will insult it
by flapping to the neighbour rhino.

My parasites not good enough for you?
Sensitive to not being known
as sensitive, it's delicate.

Its eyes easily tear-up.
I'll never say, "Those beady eyes"
because the blank stare

from that armour-plated head
means a leathery half-ton truck
is headed my way, my side of the road.

Those armoured body panels
might be scar tissue from previous
collisions, but they still protect.

MY SKUNK

is black and white
a printed sentence:
Keep your distance.

My skunk is also smell,
of course, sharp teeth,
and an undergrowth creature.

But bless my skunk for directness,
its announcement to a purpose
a black and white

night-time sentence
of don't bother me
I know what I am.

MY SQUIRREL

is a nervous magician
sponsoring the illusion
of producing food from air

its fingers so fast
as they strum the spruce cones
for their stored seeds.

My squirrel is clearly anxious:
will it save enough
for another winter?

Will Spring find
a desiccated rodent
good only for crows?

Will insomnia strike it,
the condition
its own worry worsens?

Work will reward as my squirrel
will sleep well and dreamless
wrapped in its conjurer's warmth.

MY MOOSE

sends me new poems
if clumsily on cloven hoof
and ready for disassembly,

so odd do look their parts.
My moose and its poems
are often water-logged

neither floating nor swimming
but believing there's
pasture in the muck.

I wait so eagerly
for that low bellow
which is my moose, singing.

MY RAT

is courteous,
extending its paw
to all the planet's detritus.

If politeness makes my rat
appear slick, it shrugs it off
with a whisker brush.

My rat knows that propriety
makes it plump and it's sure
there will always be garbage

and room for grateful scavengers
rejoicing in the bits
other lives have left.

MY MAMMOTH

is proud of its woolly coat
and the thick skin it's grown
being an ice-age or more dead.

It watches its glacier
slide slowly to the present
and dreams of a warm future

as it sees coming near
the light of a time
millennia from its death.

My mammoth holds its tusks
upright, challenging the ice
to let it go, now.

It will find no woolly coat,
nor skin, nor elegant tusk
readies it for its thaw.

MY HYENA

laughs at its own jokes
because they're all
funny, with perfect

timing
even if most are about
carrion and the joke

is told by teeth ripping
flesh, bloody-snouted
and very persistent.

My hyena's jokes
are thus mostly about
others already dead.

My hyena laughs.
Did I mention
timing?

MY GOPHER

knows it's all in the tunneling
the underground roads
and motels it models in clay.

My gopher worries
its dirt debris mounds
are restaurant doors

displayed to predators,
but it knows its claws
are the only map for hiding

or escape. Until scamper
from weasel crosses
the flattening highway.

MY JACK-RABBIT

favours white for winter
as does my garden
where it finds enough dry grass

to get it to Spring
if it escapes coyote
car and other calamity.

My jack-rabbit is mostly
mere tracks in the snow for me
but I read survival

to summer, when it will dress
in brown, loyal to the soil
which will then feed it green.

MY HIPPO

is river-horse
to my upstream cowboy
and I'm riding both

river and horse down the flow.
My hippo warns rivers
become waterfalls

and they have to get down
to the sea
and the end of my ride.

My hippo doesn't know
I fear less the drop
than that final dissolve.

MY COUGAR

only does what it expects;
it expects to kill
to eat and it has the strength,

the grasping claws, demolition
equipment, strong jaws
to do what it expects.

It also expects, I know,
what it kills to have expected
death;

that is, surprise at the moment
but not surprise at the event,
which just is.

MY CAMEL

is sentimental.
You can tell by the tears in its eyes,
moist as an oasis.

It's remembering the times
it ate to stuff its hump
to saddle-tightening;

it's remembering the quiet cud
under date palms as even now
it flops one foot after the other

covering privation as much as land;
and it's remembering calf-days,
breezes, near the sea

before all moving became work.
There's nothing as filling
as memory and as easy to store—

my camel prepares for deserts,
including those empty
of even sand.

MY BEAR

is bi-polar; often too tired
to look at a seal,
it just sprawls ice-belly.

A splash and it's paddling hard,
even fish and kelp
interesting and edible.

My bear's unpredictable.
I never know what I'll meet
as the next ice-berg floats by

or runs aground
on the cold shingles
of where I live.

MY ELEPHANT

is sad, as it
rides my shoulder.
I smell its savanna breath.

I should hook my elbows
over its tusks so casual
an ivory railing to stop my falling.

Except that it's on my shoulders
and waving its trunk in my face
saying, Compare noses. No, I kid,

it's saying I'm here
and I'm not going away
until you can lift me off.

MY HORSE

is mortgaged
making daily payments
with its back and muscles

but unsure when it will pay off
the balance it seems to owe
but does not recall borrowing.

My horse lives thus in debt
the permanence of which,
surprisingly, comforts.

MY GIRAFFE

doesn't exist.
Because it can't.
Impossibly long legs

afterthought of a tail
and a neck which
starves it, so long does it take

for food to get down.
Its small head, though,
on its watch-tower body

sees so much so far
it might even detect
what's real.

MY GOAT

never gets got
despite being omnivorous,
especially through its eyes.

My goat misses nothing
of passing interest, or even
of any passing at all.

My goat is the perfect reporter
except that it stops
with investigation

and never bleats what it's learned,
because it's learned all, including
it's important to keep forage to itself.

MY PIG

accomodates garbage
and wears an overcoat of mud
to warm its pink skin.

It understands rot, decay
and all that ends as soil
including its own pink skin.

My pig might have insight
—everything smells of passing time—
but when it grunts and snuffles

from swollen sleep each dawn
it smells only the light and odour
of a coming fat, permanent breakfast.

MY COW

resents that I see it
as steaks and roasts
in a leather coat.

It chews sunlight
and is the perfect
meditator,

each new mouthful of grass
a nameste from it
to its earth.

Your loss, says my cow,
if you see it merely grazing
meat from soil and root

each head dip
just another bow
for the applause of eating it.

MY ZEBRA

is unique
a pattern of different grasslands
on its side and back.

My zebra could be my fingerprint.
We are both perissodactylate
but I have much slower toes.

I wish it were as still
as the black and white
photo it is

but my zebra gallops through my dreams
scared by the predators
which hide during my days.

Uniqueness will not save it.
Not only the common die;
we all have that in common.

MY SKELETON

walks in the middle
of my body, easy in its knowledge
it will outlive me.

This makes it inflexible,
even hard on the muscles
which cling to it.

It doesn't know
there are parts it doesn't cage,
a beating heart truly untouched by it.

Yes, it cups my brain and its high
electric notions but a container
is not as important as what it contains.

My skeleton would like to leave now,
make its own clattering way in the world
but I am too possessive, too attached to let it go.

MY SELF

is all there is
to these animals
with their grunts, roars

squeals, chatter
and burrowed silence.
Some of my animals attack,

others hunker down
sure silence means death
any moment now.

None know time
beyond night and day
seasons, rain or dry

and none have history
and all have nothing to say
except: here I am, here.

MY ANIMALS

are all imagined.
I dreamt them and then awoke
to their watching me.

My animals are so various—
experiments for their time
and my time

but each its own failure
displayed here, encaged
by words, the strongest enclosure.

Envoi

There must be entrapment first
then escape, and then
this letting go.